Real Life Mindfulness

Also By Becca Anderson

◇◇◇◇◇◇◇◇◇◇◇◇◇◇◇◇◇◇◇◇◇◇◇◇◇◇◇◇◇◇◇◇

Think Happy to Stay Happy: The Awesome Power of Learned Optimism

Prayers for Hard Times: Reflections, Meditations and Inspirations for Hope & Comfort

The Book of Awesome Women: Boundary-Breakers, Freedom Fighters, Sheroes, and Female Firsts

Every Day Thankful: Blessings, Graces and Gratitudes

Real Life Mindfulness: Meditations For a Calm and Quiet Mind

Becca Anderson

Turner Publishing Company
Nashville, Tennessee
www.turnerpublishing.com

Real Life Mindfulness | Meditations for a Calm and Quiet Mind

Cover Design: Roberto Nunez
Layout & Design: Jermaine Lau

ISBN 978-1-63353-531-2

For special orders, quantity sales, course adoptions and corporate sales, please email the publisher at sales@mango.bz. For trade and wholesale sales, please contact Ingram Publisher Services at customer.service@ingramcontent.com or +1.800.509.4887.

Real Life Mindfulness: Meditations for a Calm and Quiet Mind

Library of Congress Cataloging-in-Publication has been applied for.

ISBN: (paperback) 978-1-63353-531-2 (ebook) 978-1-63353-532-9

BISAC category code OCC010000 BODY, MIND & SPIRIT / Mindfulness & Meditation SEL032000 SELF-HELP / Spiritual

Printed in the United States of America

I don't personally believe in an arrived stated of enlightenment. I feel that being human is a constant practice of return. We have moments of clarity, and then we're confused. We have incredibly sensitive periods of being awake and then we're numb. Being human is a very universal and a very personal practice of learning how to return when we can't get access to what we know.

—Mark Nepo

Contents

◇◇◇◇◇◇◇◇◇◇◇◇

Foreword

Master Mindfulness and You Will Master Your Life

People need mindfulness more than ever. The world has grown increasingly complicated and interdependent. The pace of life has accelerated tremendously and continues to move more and more quickly. Most people crave an antidote. Mindfulness provides a remedy. The practice of mindfulness simplifies, creates calm, and offers new ways to navigate the churning, uncharted waters of the digital age. What exactly is mindfulness, one may wonder. Although it's a popular term, pinpointing the exact definition of mindfulness can be difficult. Do I have to get up early? Must I do some special ritual? Mindfulness remains and has always been something simple, yet quite profound. Mindfulness in its essence means paying attention.

Mindfulness appears to be a straightforward process. Essentially it is. Yet, because life holds enormous potential for complication, continued practice and mastery of mindfulness can be challenging. There are so many distractions that can make paying attention a problematic venture, and therein lies the paradox of mindfulness. There are mundane distractions, such as to do lists, a pile of laundry, or a pebble in your shoe. There are more monumental distractions, such as natural disasters, death, accidents, or other big life changes. Mindfulness as a practice offers tips and tools to stay present, focused, and relaxed through it all, big and small.

The daily requirements of mindfulness depend on the conditions of the day. Just as a surfer must stay present, prepared, and ready to jump into action to catch a wave, a mindfulness practitioner must remain poised and ready to move with whatever influx life presents. Sometimes the waves are small, so we need to train our attention so we don't become bored. Sometimes the waves seem huge and impassable. In that case, we may need to focus on our own inner fear to get through the surf conditions of the day. Mindfulness offers us ideas and insights for staying present and alert through it all.

"Mindfulness is both a state of mind and a skill."

—Renee Metty

Mindfulness can refer to paying attention to the present moment, or it can describe meditation, as in mindfulness meditation. Open your eyes to practice mindfulness as a state of mind or close your eyes to develop the skill of meditation.

With our eyes shut, we practice mindful meditation. Mindful meditation can be practiced sitting in silence and focusing on the breath. Thoughts interrupt the practice of doing nothing; the meditator continues the practice of staying present and not distracted. Mindful meditation helps a person to harness the mind and sharpen focus, and it prepares one for staying present and attentive in daily life.

Think of the following metaphor. If life is a big party, the meditation part becomes the pre-party preparation. We clean, we organize, we plan the activities and the guest list. We get ready for the big party. Meditation becomes a way to prepare to be in the present moment for the party. We organize, sort through our thoughts, and clear the mind to make space for life.

Then on the day of the party, we engage in what I call "everyday mindfulness."

We practice being present and engaged, having fun or maybe not so much fun as the party unfolds in whatever way it unfolds. We stay awake and fully connected.

"Everyday mindfulness" doesn't require shutting your eyes. All that's needed is the focus to engage in whatever is happening around you—to see, feel, smell, notice your body, taste, and listen. You can engage in mindful walking, dancing, gardening, or just watching clouds float by. Everyday mindfulness might be washing the dishes and feeling the warm water, the soap, the sponge, the grime and grease. It's a reckoning and surrender to the mundane.

In goal-oriented activities, mindfulness means paying attention in the moment and letting go of the outcome. For this reason, more and more professional and nonprofessional athletes are embracing the tenets and philosophies of mindfulness. We are better players in sports and in life when we live mindfully. The Golden State Warriors won two NBA championships in part by embracing a mission based on mindfulness.

My early struggles sent me in search of something called mindfulness even though I had no idea what I was looking for. I grew up in a family of what I describe as nutty professors, deep thinkers who liked to debate and escape into the books they read. During our family meals, everyone had a book, magazine, or newspaper in their hands. Rather than engage in conversation, my brother and parents preferred the company of literature. Even though this was many decades ago, the behavior I saw was remarkably similar to twenty-first-century behavior. Many people engage with their digital devices at the dinner table. I recall feeling confused by this behavior. I longed for connection and presence, but I had no idea what I was looking for and I was not sure how to find it. I remember once snapping a photo of my family reading together at the dinner table. I wanted to document them all paying attention to the printed word instead of a lively conversation or even the food they ate. What I experienced as a child was very different from what I saw around most family tables at the time.

Although I didn't know anything about mindfulness, I recognized my need for something different. It wasn't that I didn't want to read or learn. I just wanted connection, focus, and attention from my family of origin as a child, and later as a teenager. I craved presence and connection. Although I know my family members loved me, focusing on the attentional moment was not a priority, especially during mealtimes.

Later when I left home, I had my own issues with being distracted and unfocused. I was carried away by daydreams, college studies, and social life. I often lost my car keys, got into minor accidents, and a few people even speculated that I was on drugs. I was in my own inner world. My own rapid mind caused me to become discombobulated. I struggled with attention and focus. I was someone who desperately needed the tools and tricks of mindfulness to lead a happier, more productive life.

After graduating from college, I found my way to a meditation class. I took up the practice whole heartedly. I felt more clear, stable, and focused than ever before. I discovered meditation as a way back to the present moment. Meditation eventually led me to the philosophical and physical practice of yoga, which increased my ability to be mindful, present, and focused in a hectic world. I felt happier than ever before and able to connect and be present with family and friends as I had always longed to be.

My daily practice goes something like this. Almost without exception, I meditate daily. Most days I meditate for twenty minutes, sometimes less, sometimes more. The important thing for me is to do it daily. Consistency is a key. I believe making mediation a daily habit trumps duration of time sitting in silence. Later, after tea and other self-care practices, I take a mindful walk with my dog. Pets can be a great contribution to a mindful life. For me, I have found having a dog helps me to be more consistent in my focus and mindful of the time passing during the day. Dogs live mindfully and in tune with nature! All animals live mindfully, for they only know the present moment. Although they sometimes eat too quickly, they know when they are hungry and let us know. Many people believe they are too busy to care for an animal. I would say this might be exactly the reason to get one. Pets force us to slow down. They motivate us to walk and spend time in nature. I often listen to podcasts while walking my dog. However, I try to walk at least three times a week in silence, taking in the world around me with my senses. I smell the scents around me on my mindful walk. I feel my feet hitting the ground and I notice my body and how it moves in space. I look at the light and see all the colors around me. I sometimes even try to taste the air, if it is pleasant. The more one taps into the senses, the more present we become.

Animals also teach us about compassion. They love unconditionally. Have you noticed that it is hard to live in the moment and be self-critical? Compassion and curiosity are essential factors of living in the moment. If I find myself upset, frustrated, or angry, I slow down and try to process. I may try some gentle or restorative yoga, especially on days when there is a lot to sort out. If I feel particularly overwhelmed, I sit down and meditate again. Another daily practice that calms my body and centers my mind is abhyanga, a mindful practice based in Ayurveda that means self-massage. In traditional abhyanga, one uses oil, such as sesame or coconut oil, sometimes infused with essential oils. Abhyanga can be as simple as massaging your own hands or feet or the entire body. The importance of abhyanga comes from its link to compassion. When we treat ourselves kindly, the rewards are great. I find that abhyanga helps me to be more self-reliant and proactive. I am taking care of myself through my own sense of loving touch and proprioception. When I care for myself with my own hands,

I take time to reflect on the sacredness and importance of me right now. I pay careful attention and am mindful of my own body and health. This is one of my favorite mindful practices.

As a yoga and meditation instructor, I look for many ways to introduce the skills and states of mindfulness. Sitting in silence, breathing, doing active or restorative yoga poses, or taking a walk are all ways to practice being mindful. One only needs to show up and be deeply engaged. The quotes in this book will help you show up mindfully. Like a little coach you can put in your pocket, these mindful quotes guide and instruct the reader to peace and presence. I often use quotes in my yoga classes that introduce the art of mindfulness. Use these words for a daily nibble of quiet and focus. Practice, practice, practice paying attention. Take these quotes and turn to them for contemplation and a deepening of your daily awakening. Use them to help you navigate the sometimes placid, occasionally murky, periodically turbulent waters of life.

Introduction: What Is Mindfulness?

◇◇◇◇◇◇◇◇◇◇◇◇◇◇◇◇◇◇◇◇◇

Mindfulness is a word that, for many, has no real, solid definition. It's all well and good to talk about paying attention to the world around you, but in real life, how practical is that, really? After all, we live in a world where we're constantly connected—connected to work, to friends, to that guy you met once in high school and who occasionally likes your tweets. What good is it to sit and observe the places you go every day when there's so much going on that you could be missing?

As many of the people in this book would tell you, practicing mindfulness really does do a lot of good. In a day and age when practically everyone is struggling with some level of anxiety and depression, mindfulness can help you refocus. It can remind you that, chances are, you have everything you really need. And if you don't, practicing mindfulness can help you to accept the reality of where you are now and to move toward what you need instead of allowing difficulties and hardships to bog you down.

Mindfulness is more than just looking around you and noticing things like the color of the walls and the feel of the chair beneath you. Mindfulness is intentionally focusing on where you are and what you're doing right now, and it's done in the small moments. Do you have a scary doctor's appointment tomorrow? Force yourself to focus on the work you're doing now. Are you distracted by Facebook while eating dinner? Put the phone down and enjoy your meal; pay attention to the unique flavors and textures of the food. Instead of waking up and immediately picking up your phone or starting your morning routine, take three minutes to sit, to breathe, to start the day right. Allow yourself time to just *be*.

Meditation—the act of sitting and focusing on your breathing, of letting thoughts and life go for just a few minutes of your day—can help you to start living with mindfulness, to start living here and now instead of next week and online. But true mindfulness happens when you're actively living life—when you're going about your day. As you travel to work, keep your phone in your pocket and notice things you don't normally pay attention to. What stores are around you at the stoplight? Is there a secret park somewhere that you never knew about? Is the sun warm and the sky blue, or is it cloudy and cold out? Look around without judging. Will complaining internally about the cold make the Earth tilt back toward the sun? Of course not. Accept the reality of what is.

Don't stop with your surroundings, though. Also pay attention to what's happening in your own heart and mind. Allow things to be what they are. When you're happy, hold on to the emotion and really feel it. When you're sad or stressed, allow yourself to be sad or stressed. Acknowledge the hardships you're facing instead of trying to push them deep down inside the dark corners of your heart. If you can allow reality to be what it is, if you can allow yourself to be who you are, you can learn how to accept anger and sadness and then let it go.

Start by giving yourself a few moments to pay attention to what's around and inside you every day. If you can, work on it at the same time every day. Be intentional. Build a habit. Soon, you'll find that you're able to focus on what you're working on a little more easily. You'll find yourself enjoying the small, individual moments that make each day unique. And you'll be able to let go of things you never thought you could just let go of.

Mindfulness is not a get-well-quick scheme. It's a new way of life.

—Elise Marie Collins

CHAPTER ONE

Pay Attention to Everything—the Whole World and Yourself—with Love and Kindness

◇◇◇◇◇◇◇◇◇◇◇◇◇◇◇◇◇◇◇◇◇◇◇◇◇

Radiate boundless love toward the entire world.

—Buddha

Mindfulness is deliberately paying full attention to what is happening around you—in your body, heart, and mind. Mindfulness is awareness without criticism or judgment.

—Hab Chozen Bays

Mindfulness has helped me succeed in almost every dimension of my life. By stopping regularly to look inward and become aware of my mental state, I stay connected to the source of my actions and thoughts and can guide them with considerably more intention.

—Dustin Moskovitz

Paying attention to and staying with finer and finer sensations within the body is one of the surest ways to steady the wandering mind.

—Ravi Ravindra

Sati–sampajanna (“Mindfulness and clear comprehension”) should be examined carefully from the point of view of the centipede who could not walk when she thought about how she moved her limbs. And from the point of view of absorption in, say artistic creation and detached observation of it. Absorption in piano playing or painting seems to be “successful” but detached observation or enjoyment of "my playing"…seems to have the centipede effect.

—Nanamoli Thera

The most fundamental aggression to ourselves, the most fundamental harm we can do to ourselves, is to remain ignorant by not having the courage and the respect to look at ourselves honestly and gently.

—Pema Chödrön

◇◇◇◇◇◇◇◇◇◇◇◇◇◇◇◇◇◇◇◇◇◇◇◇◇◇◇◇◇◇

Learn as You Go: How Should I Sit When I Meditate?

When you meditate, you don't have to sit on the floor with your legs crossed in some amazingly flexible way. In fact, if you don't normally sit on the floor or cross your legs, you should avoid doing either of those things! Instead, you can sit on a chair in an easily maintainable position, your feet flat on the floor and your back straight, but not rigid. Meditation is supposed to help you, so it's important to set yourself up for success by sitting in a comfortable position.

◇◇◇◇◇◇◇◇◇◇◇◇◇◇◇◇◇◇◇◇◇◇◇◇◇◇◇◇◇◇◇◇◇◇

Replace fear of your own inner experience with a curious, gentle, welcoming attitude—free of judgment, self-blame, and aversion.

—Melanie Greenberg

Mindfulness shows us what is happening in our bodies, our emotions, our minds, and in the world. Through mindfulness, we avoid harming ourselves and others.

—Thích Nhất Hạnh

Whatever you did today is enough. Whatever you felt today is valid. Whatever you thought today isn't to be judged. Repeat the above each day.

—Brittany Burgunder

Mindful self-compassion can be learned by anyone. It's the practice of repeatedly evoking good will toward ourselves especially when we're suffering—cultivating the same desire that all living beings have to live happily and free from suffering.

—Christopher Germer

Mindfulness: Taking a balanced approach to negative emotions so that feelings are neither suppressed nor exaggerated. We cannot ignore our pain and feel compassion for it at the same time. Mindfulness requires that we not "over-identify" with thoughts and feelings, so that we are caught up and swept away by negativity.

—Brené Brown

It's not that God, the environment, and other people cannot help us to be happy or find satisfaction. It's just that our happiness, satisfaction, and our understanding, even of God, will be no deeper than our capacity to know ourselves inwardly, to encounter the world from the deep comfort that comes from being at home in one's own skin, from an intimate familiarity with the ways of one's own mind and body.

—Jon Kabat-Zinn

◇◇◇◇◇◇◇◇◇◇◇◇◇◇◇◇◇◇◇◇◇◇◇◇◇◇◇◇◇◇◇◇◇◇◇

Engage and Immerse: Breath-Focused Meditation (1–5 Minutes)

The breath-focused meditation is typically a short meditation intended to refocus you during your day. You can do this anytime, anywhere. I usually do it when I feel particularly stressed but don't have a lot of time to meditate.

Start by sitting in a comfortable position. Take a deep breath in and let it go, slowly, gently closing your eyes, then return to breathing normally. Take a few moments to notice how your body feels. Does it feel good? Are you sore anywhere? Once you've acknowledged these feelings, allow yourself to let them go. Softly pull your focus inward to your breaths. Notice how each intake of air is different from the last. If you find yourself straying to other thoughts, gently let go of them, allow them to pass you by, and bring yourself back to the breath. Allow your breath to lead your mind instead of the other way around. Continue this for a few moments. When you're ready, slowly, gently open your eyes and continue your day.

◇◇◇◇◇◇◇◇◇◇◇◇◇◇◇◇◇◇◇◇◇◇◇◇◇◇◇◇◇◇◇◇◇◇◇

Feelings, whether of compassion or irritation, should be welcomed, recognized, and treated on an absolutely equal basis; because both are ourselves. The tangerine I am eating is me. The mustard greens I am planting are me. I plant with all my heart and mind. I clean this teapot with the kind of attention I would have were I giving the baby Buddha or Jesus a bath. Nothing should be treated more carefully than anything else.

—Thích Nhất Hạnh

In a true you-and-I relationship, we are present mindfully, nonintrusively, the way we are present with things in nature. We do not tell a birch tree it should be more like an elm. We face it with no agenda, only an appreciation that becomes participation: "I love looking at this birch" becomes "I am this birch" and then "I and this birch are opening to a mystery that transcends and holds us both."

—David Richo

It takes a little bit of mindfulness and a little bit of attention to others to be a good listener, which helps cultivate emotional nurturing and engagement.

—Deepak Chopra

With silence comes mindfulness, and thus we become better at choosing our words with kind intent before we express them.

—Alaric Hutchinson

When you open your mind, you open new doors to new possibilities for yourself and new opportunities to help others.

—Roy Bennett

Respond; don't react.

Listen; don't talk.

Think; don't assume.

—Raji Lukkoor

When you practice mindfulness, you bloom like a flower.

—Debasish Mridha

Chapter Two

You Have What You Need, Now Accept It

◇◇◇◇◇◇◇◇◇◇◇◇◇◇◇◇◇◇◇

If we could see the miracle of a single flower clearly our whole life would change.

—Buddha

The skill of mindfulness allows you to remain grounded in the present moment even when you face difficult stressors, so that your stressful feelings feel more manageable.

—Melanie Greenberg

Mindfulness means being present to whatever is happening here and now—when mindfulness is strong, there is no room left in the mind for wanting something else. With less liking and disliking of what arises, there is less pushing and pulling on the world, less defining of the threshold between self and other, resulting in a reduced construction of self. As the influence of self diminishes, suffering diminishes in proportion.

—Andrew Olendzki

In meditation we discover our inherent restlessness. Sometimes we get up and leave. Sometimes we sit there but our bodies wiggle and squirm and our minds go far away. This can be so uncomfortable that we feel it's impossible to stay. Yet this feeling can teach us not just about ourselves but what it is to be human…we really don't want to stay with the nakedness of our present experience.

—Pema Chödrön

It's like wearing gloves every time we touch something, and then, forgetting we chose to put them on, we complain that nothing feels quite real. Our challenge each day is not to get dressed to face the world but to unglove ourselves so that the doorknob feels cold and the car handle feels wet and the kiss goodbye feels like the lips of another being, soft and unrepeatable.

—Mark Nepo

There is something wonderfully bold and liberating about saying yes to our entire imperfect and messy life.

—Tara Brach

◇◇◇◇◇◇◇◇◇◇◇◇◇◇◇◇◇◇◇◇◇◇◇◇◇◇◇◇◇◇◇◇◇◇

Learn as You Go: How Should I Breathe When I Meditate?

Meditation often begins with a deep intake of breath and a long exhalation. But you don't have to keep breathing that way after you've started! The deep breath at the beginning is intended to refocus yourself on the moment, on what you're doing now—namely, the meditation practice. Once you're refocused, you should breathe normally, allowing your body to take care of itself again while you meditate.

◇◇◇◇◇◇◇◇◇◇◇◇◇◇◇◇◇◇◇◇◇◇◇◇◇◇◇◇◇◇◇◇

The essence of bravery is being without self-deception.

—Pema Chödrön

Acknowledging the pain and the suffering that take place inside you, and allowing the feelings, will take time, but this new way of handling these feelings will change the way you relate to you and to the outside world.

—Kelly Martin

In fact, when you're mindful, you actually feel irritation more keenly. However, once you unburden yourself from the delusion that people are deliberately trying to screw you, it's easier to stop getting carried away.

—Dan Harris

By learning to allow different types of discomfort to simply stay in the room with you, without your scrambling for a button to push (real or metaphorical), you make discomfort matter less.

The pool of things you're afraid of shrinks. It becomes a lot less important to control circumstances, because you know you can handle moments of uncertainty or awkwardness or disappointment without an escape plan.

—David Cain

By identifying impermanence as a fundamental characteristic of existence itself, rather than a problem to be solved, the Buddhists are encouraging us to let go our hold on illusory solidity and learn to swim freely in the sea of change.

—Andrew Olendzki

◇◇◇◇◇◇◇◇◇◇◇◇◇◇◇◇◇◇◇◇◇◇◇◇◇◇◇◇◇◇◇◇◇◇

Engage and Immerse: Quiet Observation Meditation (5–15 minutes)

The quiet observation meditation is intended to bring you back to where you are and what you have already, all round you. I use it when I want to remind myself just how much life has given me, to appreciate it in a new and greater way.

Sit or stand in a maintainable, comfortable position. Begin by taking a deep breath in, and as you breathe out, slowly close your eyes. Take a few regular breaths and focus on your breathing, how your body moves with each intake, how your muscles soften each time you exhale. When you are ready, gently let go of that focus. Take a few moments to listen. What do you hear? Is there a faint buzzing from machinery? Can you hear the wind outside? Are people talking nearby? Be careful to observe your surroundings without judgment. When you are ready, open your eyes and slowly examine what you can see. Notice the details of every object around you. Acknowledge the existence of each and every thing that you can see and hear.

When you have finished, let go of that observational focus and mindfully resume your day.

◇◇◇◇◇◇◇◇◇◇◇◇◇◇◇◇◇◇◇◇◇◇◇◇◇◇◇◇◇◇◇◇◇◇◇

If you meditate in perfect peace and then flash someone an irritable look because they make noise or their child cries, you are entirely missing the point.

—Khandro Rinpoche

It stands to reason that anyone who learns to live well will die well. The skills are the same: being present in the moment, and humble, and brave, and keeping a sense of humor.

—Victoria Moran

You can't stop the waves, but you can learn to surf.

—Jon Kabat-Zinn

One does not become enlightened by imagining figures of light, but by making the darkness conscious. The latter procedure, however, is disagreeable and therefore not popular.

—C. G. Jung

You might be tempted to avoid the messiness of daily living for the tranquility of stillness and peacefulness. This of course would be an attachment to stillness, and like any strong attachment, it leads to delusion. It arrests development and short-circuits the cultivation of wisdom.

—Jon Kabat-Zinn

If you live the sacred and despise the ordinary, you are still bobbing in the ocean of delusion.

—Linji Yixuan

Chapter Three

Live in the Moment as If It Were the Last Moment You Had

◇◇◇◇◇◇◇◇◇◇◇

Do not dwell in the past, do not dream of the future, concentrate the mind on the present moment.

—Buddha

Start living right here, in each present moment. When we stop dwelling on the past or worrying about the future, we're open to rich sources of information we've been missing out on—information that can keep us out of the downward spiral and poised for a richer life.

—Mark Williams

What is the date? What is the time?… Great, that's what Now is. And every second, your "Now" changes. Because all we have is Now. We are continuously living in the Now. Not yesterday, not tomorrow, but Now. Today. The present. And I need you to live in it. To truly appreciate it. To breathe and feel yourself breathing.

—S.R. Crawford

It goes against the grain to stay present. These are the times when only gentleness and a sense of humor can give us the strength to settle down… so whenever we wander off, we gently encourage ourselves to "stay" and settle down. Are we experiencing restlessness? Stay! Are fear and loathing out of control? Stay! Aching knees and throbbing back? Stay! What's for lunch? Stay! I can't stand this another minute! Stay!

—Pema Chödrön

We have only now, only this single eternal moment opening and unfolding before us, day and night.

—Jack Kornfield

If you are doing mindfulness meditation, you are doing it with your ability to attend to the moment.

—Daniel Goleman

Learn as You Go: How Long Should I Meditate For?

You may have noticed that each Engage and Immerse meditation has a suggested amount of time in parentheses next to the title. These are merely suggestions, to give you an idea of how long each meditation may take when you start. That being said, you can meditate for as long or as little as you want. Do you only have two minutes to meditate on your break? Meditate for two minutes. Do you want to meditate for an hour before or after work? Meditate for an hour. Meditation is ultimately for your well-being, so you get to decide how long you do it for.

◇◇◇◇◇◇◇◇◇◇◇◇◇◇◇◇◇◇◇◇◇◇◇◇◇◇◇◇◇◇◇

If you want to conquer the anxiety of life, live in the moment, live in the breath.

—Amit Ray

Do not encumber your mind with useless thoughts. What good does it do to brood on the past or anticipate the future? Remain in the simplicity of the present moment.

—Dilgo Khyentse Rinpoche

If you aren't in the moment, you are either looking forward to uncertainty, or back to pain and regret.

—Jim Carrey

The only thing that is ultimately real about your journey is the step that you are taking at this moment. That's all there ever is.

—Eckhart Tolle

Few of us ever live in the present. We are forever anticipating what is to come or remembering what has gone.

—Louis L'Amour

The present moment is the only time over which we have dominion.

—Thích Nhất Hạnh

You have to remember one life, one death–this one! To enter fully the day, the hour, the moment whether it appears as life or death, whether we catch it on the inbreath or outbreath, requires only a moment, this moment. And along with it all the mindfulness we can muster, and each stage of our ongoing birth, and the confident joy of our inherent luminosity.

—Stephen Levine

◇◇◇◇◇◇◇◇◇◇◇◇◇◇◇◇◇◇◇◇◇◇◇◇◇◇◇◇◇◇◇◇◇◇◇

Engage and Immerse: Mindful Eating Meditation (10–20 minutes)

The mindful eating meditation is intended to help you to become mindful in your day-to-day activities and tasks. I especially like to do this meditation when I've had a day full of planning or worrying about the future because it grounds me back into the present

This meditation can be done during a meal or a snack, which should be prepared before you start. Begin by taking a deep breath in and letting it out, drawing your mind to the present moment and each individual action you take during it. Then you may start to eat your meal. As you eat, focus on exactly what you're doing while you're doing it. If you have to open a container, acknowledge the container, pay attention to the action of opening it. If you are using utensils, notice the feel of the utensils in your hands, the weight and motion of rising and falling when you bring food from the dish to your mouth. With each bite, savor the flavors and textures of the food. Allow them to be what they are without judging them. It does not matter whether you like or dislike what you are eating—either way, the food will sustain you. Continue this meditation until you have finished eating.

◇◇◇◇◇◇◇◇◇◇◇◇◇◇◇◇◇◇◇◇◇◇◇◇◇◇◇◇◇◇◇◇◇◇◇◇

We speculate, dream, strategize, and plan for these "conditions of happiness" we want to have in the future; and we continually chase after that future, even while we sleep. We may have fears about the future because we don't know how it's going to turn out, and these worries and anxieties keep us from enjoying being here now.

—Thích Nhất Hạnh

Perfection of character is this: to live each day as if it were your last, without frenzy, without apathy, without pretense.

—Marcus Aurelius

Throughout this life, you can never be certain of living long enough to take another breath.

—Huang Po

It's only when we truly know and understand that we have a limited time on earth—and that we have no way of knowing when our time is up—that we will begin to live each day to the fullest, as if it was the only one we had.

—Elisabeth Kübler-Ross

Do every act of your life as though it were the very last act of your life.

—Marcus Aurelius

Most people treat the present moment as if it were an obstacle that they need to overcome. Since the present moment is life itself, it is an insane way to live.

—Eckhart Tolle

Chapter Four:

See the Beauty That Is Already Present in the Little Things All Around You

◇◇◇◇◇◇◇◇◇◇◇◇◇◇

Every experience, no matter how bad it seems, holds within it a blessing of some kind. The goal is to find it.

—Buddha

Each step along the Buddha's path to happiness requires practicing mindfulness until it becomes part of your daily life.

—Henepola Gunaratana

Our culture encourages us to plan every moment and fill our schedules with one activity and obligation after the next, with no time to just be. But the human body and mind require downtime to rejuvenate. I have found my greatest moments of joy and peace just sitting in silence, and then I take that joy and peace with me out into the world.

—Holly Mosier

Be happy in the moment, that's enough. Each moment is all we need, not more.

—Mother Teresa

This is the real secret of life—to be completely engaged with what you are doing in the here and now. And instead of calling it work, realize it is play.

—Alan Watts

◇◇◇◇◇◇◇◇◇◇◇◇◇◇◇◇◇◇◇◇◇◇◇◇◇◇◇◇◇◇◇◇◇◇◇

Learn as You Go: When and Where Should I Meditate?

As you may already know, meditation can be done anytime and anywhere. That being said, if you want to build a lasting habit, you should try to meditate at approximately the same time and place each day. This way, your brain will start to associate that time and place with meditating and will be prepared when you get there.

◇◇◇◇◇◇◇◇◇◇◇◇◇◇◇◇◇◇◇◇◇◇◇◇◇◇◇◇◇◇◇◇◇◇◇

To be sensual, I think, is to respect and rejoice in the force of life, of life itself, and to be present in all that one does, from the effort of loving to the breaking of bread.

—James Baldwin

The present moment is filled with joy and happiness. If you are attentive, you will see it.

—Thích Nhất Hạnh

The only way to live is by accepting each minute as an unrepeatable miracle.

—Tara Brach

The things that matter most in our lives are not fantastic or grand. They are moments when we touch one another.

—Jack Kornfield

The moment one gives close attention to anything, even a blade of grass, it becomes a mysterious, awesome, indescribably magnificent world in itself.

—Henry Miller

Seek and see all the marvels around you. You will get tired of looking at yourself alone, and that fatigue will make you deaf and blind to everything else.

—Don Juan

◇◇◇◇◇◇◇◇◇◇◇◇◇◇◇◇◇◇◇◇◇◇◇◇◇◇◇◇◇◇◇◇◇◇◇

Engage and Immerse: Nature-Focused Meditative Walk (5–15 minutes)

The nature-focused meditative walk is intended to remind you of all the natural beauty that exists around you every day. I like to do it whenever I've spend much of the day (or the week) inside, especially if I've been focused primarily on difficult tasks or complaints.

Begin by standing still outside. Take a deep breath in and let it out, then take your first step, walking and breathing normally, not too fast and not too slow. As you walk, take notice of your surroundings. Look for pockets of nature—is grass peeking through the cracks in the sidewalk? Are there trees and bushes anywhere? How about flowers? Look for green plants, brown earth, blue or gray sky. Is it cold or warm? Bright or cloudy? Continue your walk and observe your surroundings without judging them: let them be what they are.

◇◇◇◇◇◇◇◇◇◇◇◇◇◇◇◇◇◇◇◇◇◇◇◇◇◇◇◇◇◇◇◇◇

Life is not lost by dying; life is lost
minute by minute, day by dragging day,
in all the small uncaring ways.

—Stephen Vincent Benet

Mindfulness helps us freeze the frame so that we can become aware of our sensations and experiences as they are, without the distorting coloration of socially conditioned responses or habitual reactions.

—Henepola Gunaratana

Rejoicing in ordinary things is not sentimental or trite. It actually takes guts.

—Pema Chödrön

It's a funny thing about life, once you begin to take note of the things you are grateful for, you begin to lose sight of the things that you lack.

—Germany Kent

Looking at beauty in the world, is the first step of purifying the mind.

—Amit Ray

Chapter Five

Practice Mindfulness with Understanding and Intentionality; It Brings Wisdom

◇◇◇◇◇◇◇◇◇◇◇◇◇◇◇◇◇◇◇◇

Three things cannot be long hidden: the sun, the moon, and the truth.

—Buddha

Wherever you decide to go, proceed with your mind.

—Amitav Chowdhury

Everything is created twice, first in the mind and then in reality.

—Roshan Sharma

The key to creating the mental space before responding is mindfulness. Mindfulness is a way of being present: paying attention to and accepting what is happening in our lives. It helps us to be aware of and step away from our automatic and habitual reactions to our everyday experiences.

—Elizabeth Thornton

Buddhist mindfulness is about the present, but I also think it's about being real. Being awake to everything. Feeling like nothing can hurt you if you can look it straight on.

—Krista Tippett

If someone comes along and shoots an arrow into your heart, it's fruitless to stand there and yell at the person. It would be much better to turn your attention to the fact that there's an arrow in your heart.

—Pema Chödrön

◇◇◇◇◇◇◇◇◇◇◇◇◇◇◇◇◇◇◇◇◇◇◇◇◇◇◇◇◇◇◇

Learn as You Go: How Often Should I Meditate?

If you're trying to build a habit and improve your mindfulness, you should meditate at least once a day. However, if that is too stressful, don't force it! Like I've said before, meditating is for you—if you can't meditate every day without losing the benefits of practicing meditation, do it when you can. Of course,

there's no need to limit yourself
to meditating only once per day,
either—feel free to do it as often
as you want to.

◇◇◇◇◇◇◇◇◇◇◇◇◇◇◇◇◇◇◇◇◇◇◇◇◇◇◇◇◇◇◇◇◇◇◇

In any moment of time, you have three paths to choose from. You stand for something, you stand against something, or you drop both, and walk with your inner truth.

—Roshan Sharma

We need never be bound by the limitations of our previous or current thinking, nor are we ever locked into being the person we used to be, or think we are.

—Allan Lokos

Open the window of your mind. Allow the fresh air, new lights and new truths to enter.

—Amit Ray

Mindfulness isn't about ridding yourself of thoughts. It's more about being aware and letting those thoughts pass through you, so you can see what, if any, value they have for you. Thoughts

are an illusion but some of them
are enlightening.

—Nanette Mathews

Think of the old cliché about the mind being "an excellent servant but a terrible master." This, like many clichés, so lame & banal on the surface, actually expresses a great & terrible truth.

—David Foster Wallace

◇◇◇◇◇◇◇◇◇◇◇◇◇◇◇◇◇◇◇◇◇◇◇◇◇◇◇◇◇◇◇◇◇◇

Engage and Immerse: Inward-Focused Meditative Walk (5–6 minutes)

The inward-focused meditative walk is intended to use the movement of your body while walking as a focus for your mind. I like to do it when I've been sitting still all day, so sitting more to meditate is difficult and distraction-filled.

Begin by standing still in a safe location. Take a deep breath in and allow your eyes to slowly close as you breathe out, then breathe normally. Focus on the weight of your body transferring to the ground. Notice the small movements you normally make without thinking, the shifts that help you maintain balance. Once you feel grounded, slowly open your eyes and take your first step. Walk normally—not too slow, not too fast. As you begin walking, focus on the sensations of your feet as they meet the ground. Notice how your weight transfers, the textures that rub against each foot as you take a step.

When you're ready, slowly bring your focus upward to your legs. Notice how your ankles and knees are bending, how your leg muscles expand and contract. How the fabric around your legs feels as it shifts along with your pace. When you're ready, raise your focus to your torso. Pay attention to the small twists and turns it makes as you're walking, to the weight of your top on your body. Over time, expand this focus to include your arms. Are they swinging? If so, how far? Do they feel heavy or light? After you feel content with how you have acknowledged and appreciated each part of your body, shift your focus to your head. Notice how you're holding it and release any tension in your neck or in the rest of your body. Allow yourself to relax and enjoy the walk. When you're ready, gently let go of your inward focus and continue with your day.

◇◇◇◇◇◇◇◇◇◇◇◇◇◇◇◇◇◇◇◇◇◇◇◇◇◇◇◇◇◇◇◇

Use every distraction as an object of meditation and they cease to be distractions.

—Mingyur Rinpoche

You must have hope in a better future and have faith in this hope. But then you must forget your hope and focus on this moment now.

—Kamand Kojouri

Reality is only an agreement—today is always today.

—Zen Proverb

The mind is capable of the highest wisdom. It can experience love and compassion, as well as anger. It can understand history, philosophy, and mathematics—and remember what's on the grocery list. The mind is truly like a wish-fulfilling jewel. With an untrained mind, the thought process is said to be like a wild and blind horse: erratic and out of control.

—Sakyong Mipham

Knowledge does not mean mastering a great quantity of different information, but understanding the nature of mind. This knowledge can penetrate each one of our thoughts and illuminate each one of our perceptions.

—Matthieu Ricard

Chapter Six:

To Be Mindful Is to Be Objective, Non-Judgmental

◇◇◇◇◇◇◇◇◇◇◇◇◇◇◇◇◇◇◇◇◇◇◇

Happiness or sorrow—whatever befalls you, walk on untouched, unattached.

—Buddha

Central to our work and our goal of finding solutions to global problems is the concept of mindfulness, a technique for focusing attention objectively on the here and now.

—Goldie Hawn

Mindfulness is simply being aware of what is happening right now without wishing it were different; enjoying the pleasant without holding on when it changes (which it will); being with the unpleasant without fearing it will always be this way (which it won't).

—James Baraz

As we encounter new experiences with a mindful and wise attention, we discover that one of three things will happen to our new experience: it will go away, it will stay the same, or it will get more intense. Whatever happens does not really matter.

—Jack Kornfield

The ultimate experience of being mindful occurs when we forget about everything, even the mindful self and doing. In that mode we are full of energy, utterly self-generated.

—Sang H. Kim

Mindfulness is wordless. Mindfulness is meeting the moment as it is, moment after moment after moment, wordlessly attending to our experiencing as it actually is. It is opening to not just the fragments of our lives that we like or dislike or view as important, but the whole of our experiencing.

—White Wind Zen Community

◇◇◇◇◇◇◇◇◇◇◇◇◇◇◇◇◇◇◇◇◇◇◇◇◇◇◇◇◇◇◇◇◇◇

Learn as You Go: What Expectations Should I Have for Meditation?

None! If you go into meditation with certain expectations in mind, you may feel pressured in ways meditation is not built for. Since everyone is different, everyone will have different results from meditation, and that's okay. But it's important not to have too many expectations, because if you do, you may find that you're not satisfied with the results your seeing, and you may miss the small, day-to-day improvements that meditation is helping you make.

◇◇

The best way to capture moments is to pay attention. This is how we cultivate mindfulness.

—Jon Kabat-Zinn

Mindfulness is living in the moment without judging it.

—Debasish Mridha

Being mindful means that we suspend judgment for a time, set aside our immediate goals for the future, and take in the present moment as it is rather than as we would like it to be.

—Mark Williams

Nowadays, mindfulness has become a catch-all word, but the general principle of trying to be more conscious and aware in our daily life is very important. Along with this, it's helpful to contemplate some of the mind training verses which are designed to take and transform all of the problems we experience.

—Tenzin Palmo

Most of us take for granted that time flies, meaning that it passes too quickly. But in the mindful state, time doesn't really pass at all. There is only a single instant of time that keeps renewing itself over and over with infinite variety.

—Deepak Chopra

◇◇◇◇◇◇◇◇◇◇◇◇◇◇◇◇◇◇◇◇◇◇◇◇◇◇◇◇◇◇◇◇◇◇◇

Engage and Immerse: Day Scan Meditation (5–6 minutes)

The day scan meditation is intended to help you process your day and prepare for sleep. I especially like to do this meditation after a long, exhausting day, or perhaps after a day where I've felt particularly unproductive or failed at something I'd been working toward for a while.

Begin this meditation in your bed, in the same position you intend to fall asleep in. Take a deep breath in, a deep breath out, and as you breathe out, gently close your eyes. For a moment, focus on your breathing only. Prepare yourself to observe without judgment, to recap without having any opinion, and remember that in five or six minutes, you want to go through your entire day.

Then begin. Start with the morning routine, remembering this morning's unique occurrences, and continue throughout the rest of the day quickly. Remember that you are not in a rush; rather, you are merely acknowledging the day's events, so you do not want to spend too much time on anything, you don't want to give yourself time to judge it or wallow in it. The purpose of this meditation is not to dwell on the day's hardships or joys, but rather to allow them to have been, to allow them to have had meaning in their moments, to process them, and then to let them go.

◇◇◇◇◇◇◇◇◇◇◇◇◇◇◇◇◇◇◇◇◇◇◇◇◇◇◇◇◇◇◇◇◇◇◇

What I must do, is all that concerns me, not what the people think. This rule, equally arduous in actual and in intellectual life, may serve for the whole distinction between greatness and meanness. It is the harder, because you will always find those who think they know what is your duty better than you know it.

—Ralph Waldo Emerson

Mindfulness is the aware, balanced acceptance of the present experience.

It isn't more complicated than that. It is opening to or receiving the present moment, pleasant or unpleasant, just as it is, without either clinging to it or rejecting it.

—Sylvia Boorstein

Mindfulness is like a microscope; it is neither an offensive nor defensive weapon in relation to the germs we observe through it. The function of the microscope is just to clearly present what is there.

—Chogyam Trungpa

Mindfulness is the act of being intensely aware of what you're sensing and feeling at every moment—without interpretation or judgment.

—Mayo Clinic

Suffering usually relates to wanting things to be different than they are.

—Allan Lokos

Chapter Seven:

Mindfulness Is More than Just Awareness; It Is Intentional Awareness, and It Needs to Be Practiced

◇◇◇◇◇◇◇◇◇◇◇◇◇◇◇◇◇◇◇◇

To enjoy good health, to bring true happiness to one's family, to bring peace to all, one must first discipline and control one's own mind.

—Buddha

The art of living...is neither careless drifting on the one hand nor fearful clinging to the past on the other. It consists in being sensitive to each moment, in regarding it as utterly new and unique, in having the mind open and wholly receptive.

—Alan Watts

Mindful awareness, as we will see, actually involves more than just simply being aware: It involves being aware of aspects of the mind itself. Instead of being on automatic and mindless, mindfulness helps us awaken, and by reflecting on the mind we are enabled to make choices and thus change becomes possible.

—Daniel J. Siegel

Mindfulness isn't just about knowing that you're hearing something, seeing something, or even observing that you're having a particular feeling. It's about doing so in a certain way—with balance and equanimity, and without judgment. Mindfulness is the practice of paying attention in a way that creates space for insight.

—Sharon Salzberg

Every time we become aware of a thought, as opposed to being lost in a thought, we experience that opening of the mind.

—Joseph Goldstein

The purpose of meditation practice is not enlightenment; it is to pay attention even at unextraordinary times, to be of present, nothing-but-the-present, to bear this mindfulness of now into each event of ordinary life.

—Peter Matthiessen

◇◇◇◇◇◇◇◇◇◇◇◇◇◇◇◇◇◇◇◇◇◇◇◇◇◇◇◇◇◇◇◇◇◇

Learn as You Go: Do I Have to Meditate the Same Way Every Day?

The short answer: no, you do not. There's a reason why there are so many different types of meditation. Each day is unique, so you may find that being flexible in how you meditate will help you to get the most out of the practice. However, you may also find that you gravitate toward the same kind of meditation every day, and that's okay too. Each person is different,

so each person's meditative
practices will look different.

◇◇◇◇◇◇◇◇◇◇◇◇◇◇◇◇◇◇◇◇◇◇◇◇◇◇◇◇◇◇◇◇◇◇

Mindfulness means paying attention in a particular way; On purpose, in the present moment, and non-judgmentally.

—Jon Kabat-Zinn

As with any form of mental self-improvement, you must learn to turn your gaze inward, concentrate on processes that usually run automatically, and try to wrest control of them so that you can apply them more mindfully.

—Steven Pinker

In Tibet, we have a traditional image, the wind horse, which represents a balanced relationship between the wind and the mind. The horse represents wind and movement. On its saddle rides a precious jewel. That jewel is our mind.... We experience the mind as moving all the time—suddenly darting off, thinking about one thing and another, being happy, being sad. If we haven't trained our mind, the wild horse takes us wherever it wants to go.

—Sakyong Mipham

Say that the moment is a combination of thought; sensation; the voice of the sea. Waste, deadness, come from the inclusion of things that don't belong to the moment; this appalling narrative business of the realist: getting on from lunch to dinner: it is false, unreal, merely conventional.

—Virginia Woolf

Practice is this life, and realization is this life, and this life is revealed right here and now.

—Maezumi Roshi

Tethered to our smart phones, we are too caught up and distracted to take the time necessary to sort through complexity or to locate submerged purpose. In our urgent rush to get "there," we are going everywhere but being nowhere. Far too busy managing with transactive speed, we rarely step back to lead with transformative significance.

—Kevin Cashman

◇◇◇◇◇◇◇◇◇◇◇◇◇◇◇◇◇◇◇◇◇◇◇◇◇◇◇◇◇◇◇◇◇◇◇◇

Engage and Immerse: Mantra Meditation (5–20 minutes)

Mantra meditation is intended to use sounds, words, and phrases to refocus you. I like to do mantra meditation when I can't seem to escape all of my thoughts and worries about the future or the past.

For this meditation, you must come up with a word or phrase that you will repeat over and over again. This will be your mantra. One of the traditional words used is "Ohm," but it could be anything, secular or non, spiritual or non. Remember, though, that the word, sound, or phrase you use will replace your thoughts, so it should be chosen carefully, as it will be your focus for the entirety of your meditation and perhaps even for a period afterwards.

Begin by sitting in a comfortable position. Take a deep breath in and let it out, slowly closing your eyes or allowing your visual focus to blur. Then begin your mantra. Repeat your chosen mantra slowly in your mind. You can repeat it silently or murmur or whisper it quietly out loud. Focus all of your mind, all of your energy, on your mantra, allowing it to consume your every thought. You can do this a certain number of times, using a method to track your number that does not involve focusing on counting, such as moving beads along a necklace. Or, you can do this for a set amount of time, setting a non-obtrusive, mild timer that will alert you to when your meditation is finished. When you are done, take a deep breath in, and as you let it out, allow yourself to refocus on the world around you and mindfully continue your day.

◇◇◇◇◇◇◇◇◇◇◇◇◇◇◇◇◇◇◇◇◇◇◇◇◇◇◇◇◇◇◇◇◇◇

When you do something, you should burn yourself up completely, like a good bonfire, leaving no trace of yourself.

—Shunryu Suzuki

Do not force your mind to get rid of random thoughts, because your brain is simply not capable of doing so. Instead, when you sit to practice meditation, let the thoughts come and go, just don't serve them tea. Over time, that background noise inside your head will disappear.

—Abhijit Naskar

Meditation is a microcosm, a model, a mirror. The skills we practice when we sit are transferable to the rest of our lives.

—Sharon Salzberg

What you feed your mind, will lead your life.

—Kemi Sogunle

Mindfulness means being aware of how you're deploying your attention and making decisions about it, and not letting the tweet or the buzzing of your BlackBerry call your attention.

—Howard Rheingold

The mind is just like a muscle—the more you exercise it, the stronger it gets and the more it can expand.

—Idowu Koyenikan

The body benefits from movement, and the mind benefits from stillness.

—Sakyong Mipham

Chapter Eight:

◇◇◇◇◇◇◇◇◇◇◇◇◇◇◇◇◇◇

Peace and Happiness Come from Within—Come from the Heart

◇◇◇◇◇◇◇◇◇◇◇◇◇◇◇◇◇◇◇◇

Peace comes from within. Do not seek it without.

—Buddha

Mindfulness meditation doesn't change life. Life remains as fragile and unpredictable as ever. Meditation changes the heart's capacity to accept life as it is. It teaches the heart to be more accommodating, not by beating it into submission, but by making it clear that accommodation is a gratifying choice.

—Sylvia Boorstein

The practice of mindfulness begins in the small, remote cave of your unconscious mind and blossoms with the sunlight of your conscious life, reaching far beyond the people and places you can see.

—Earon Davis

Step outside for a while—calm your mind. It is better to hug a tree than to bang your head against a wall continually.

—Rasheed Ogunlaru

When you focus and accept the current moment with love, faith, and joyfulness, you are practicing mindfulness. That is better than controlling the universe.

—Debasish Mridha

Eventually it will become quiet enough so that you can simply watch the heart begin to react, and let go before the mind starts. At some point in the journey it all becomes heart, not mind.... The mind doesn't even get a chance to start up because you let go at the heart level.

—Michael Singer

◇◇◇◇◇◇◇◇◇◇◇◇◇◇◇◇◇◇◇◇◇◇◇◇◇◇◇◇◇◇◇◇◇

Learn as You Go: Do I Have to Close My Eyes When I Meditate?

Many people, especially at first, find that closing their eyes during meditation can help them to avoid distractions. Most of the meditations in this book, therefore, begin with having you close your eyes, even if just for a moment. However, if you find that you are able to focus without closing your eyes, feel free to keep them open.

◇◇◇◇◇◇◇◇◇◇◇◇◇◇◇◇◇◇◇◇◇◇◇◇◇◇◇◇◇◇◇

Your vision will become clear only when you look into your heart. Who looks outside, dreams. Who looks inside, awakens.

—Carl Jung

Rather than fretting about the past or worrying about the future, the aim is to experience life as it unfolds moment by moment. This simple practice is immensely powerful. As we rush through our lives, mindfulness encourages us to stop constantly striving for something new or better and to embrace acceptance and gratitude. This allows us to tap into the joy and wonder in our lives, and to listen to the wisdom of our hearts.

—Anna Barnes

In the end, just three things matter:
How well we have lived
How well we have loved
How well we have learned to let go

—Jack Kornfield

Sometimes you need to sit lonely on the floor in a quiet room in order to hear your own voice and not let it drown in the noise of others.

—Charlotte Eriksson

◇◇◇◇◇◇◇◇◇◇◇◇◇◇◇◇◇◇◇◇◇◇◇◇◇◇◇◇◇◇◇◇◇◇◇◇◇

Engage and Immerse: Loving Kindness Meditation (10–20 minutes)

The loving kindness meditation is intended to draw your heart into your meditation and to show love toward everyone, yourself included. I like to do it when I've had a day full of irritation or anger, especially if other people were the subjects of my negative emotions.

Sit in a comfortable position. Begin by taking a deep breath. As you breathe out, gently close your eyes, and then continue to breathe normally. Think of yourself, focusing on your heart, not your mind, and feel the love coming from yourself. Begin silently with positive "May I..." statements of well-being and kindness for yourself (examples below). Once you have spent a good moment on yourself, think of a close friend or relative and continue making silent statements, this time starting with "May you..." Spend the same amount of time on this person as you did on yourself; every person is equal and deserves equal attention, equal love.

Once you have finished, progress to someone you may not know very well but do not have negative feelings toward, again spending an equal amount of time generating kind and loving "May you…" statements. Next, progress to someone who you may have difficulty loving in an active sense, spending the same amount of time on them, as well. Finally, imagine the world as a whole, with all of its people in it, all of its equally valuable beings, and continue making "May you…" statements.

This last moment may be longer than those spent on single

individuals (as this last moment includes a plethora of equal sentient creatures and not just one), or it may last the same amount of time as all of your previous moments.

Some examples of "May I/you…" statements:

May I/you be free from harm.

May I/you be happy.

May I/you live with ease.

May I/you be free from physical or mental suffering.

◇◇◇◇◇◇◇◇◇◇◇◇◇◇◇◇◇◇◇◇◇◇◇◇◇◇◇◇◇◇◇◇◇◇◇

Happiness is your nature. It is not wrong to desire it. What is wrong is seeking it outside when it is inside.

—Ramana Maharshi

The idea has come to me that what I want now to do is to saturate every atom. I mean to eliminate all waste, deadness, superfluity: to give the moment whole; whatever it includes.

—Virginia Woolf

Two thoughts cannot coexist at the same time: if the clear light of mindfulness is present, there is no room for mental twilight.

—Nyanaponika Thera

Mindfulness is a quality that's always there. It's an illusion that there's a meditation and post-meditation period, which I always find amusing, because you're either mindful or you're not.

—Richard Gere

The pathos of the human life teaches one that idolatry of the ego is a sham. Only by living in harmonious accord with the entire world can a person distill happiness that flows from cultivating a state of mindfulness.

—Kilroy J. Oldster

Life is a dance. Mindfulness is witnessing that dance.

—Amit Ray

Chapter Nine:

◇◇◇◇◇◇◇◇◇◇◇◇◇◇◇◇◇◇

CHAPTER NINE

Instead of Looking to the Future, Look at Where You Are Now: You Have All You Need

◇◇◇◇◇◇◇◇◇◇◇◇

Be where you are, otherwise you will miss your life.

—Buddha

Each place is the right place—the place where I now am can be a sacred space.

—Ravi Ravindra

The standard way of reducing stress in our culture is to put as much energy as possible into trying to arrive at a moment that matches our preferences. This ensures that we feel some level of stress until we get there (assuming we ever will) and worse, it makes the present moment into an unacceptable place to be.

—David Cain

Surrender to what is. Let go of what was. Have faith in what will be.

—Sonia Ricotti

Drink your tea slowly and reverently, as if it is the axis on which the world Earth revolves—slowly, evenly, without rushing toward the future.

—Thích Nhất Hạnh

If you're always racing to the next moment, what happens to the one you're in? Slow down and enjoy the moment you're in and live your life to the fullest.

—Nanette Mathews

◇◇◇◇◇◇◇◇◇◇◇◇◇◇◇◇◇◇◇◇◇◇◇◇◇◇◇◇◇◇◇◇◇

Learn as You Go: What's the Best Form of Meditation?

The short answer: there is none. Meditation is ultimately a tool to help you gain mindfulness in your entire life. Each person will find that a slightly different form or style of meditation helps them the best—or perhaps they will find that they like different types for different purposes. On your journey, you get to discover what works best for you.

◇◇◇◇◇◇◇◇◇◇◇◇◇◇◇◇◇◇◇◇◇◇◇◇◇◇◇◇◇◇◇◇◇◇◇◇◇

The mind in its natural state can be compared to the sky, covered by layers of cloud which hide its true nature.

—Kalu Rinpoche

Like a child standing in a beautiful park with his eyes shut tight, there's no need to imagine trees, flowers, deer, birds, and sky; we merely need to open our eyes and realize what is already here, who we already are—as soon as we stop pretending we're small or unholy.

—Bo Lozoff

Expectation has brought me disappointment. Disappointment has brought me wisdom. Acceptance, gratitude and appreciation have brought me joy and fulfilment.

—Rasheed Ogunlaru

It is easy in the world to live after the world's opinion; it is easy in solitude to live after our own; but the great man is he who in the midst of the crowd keeps with perfect sweetness the independence of solitude.

—Ralph Waldo Emerson

◇◇◇◇◇◇◇◇◇◇◇◇◇◇◇◇◇◇◇◇◇◇◇◇◇◇◇◇◇◇◇◇◇

Engage and Immerse: Anxiety and Relaxation Meditation (5–10 Minutes)

The anxiety and relaxation meditation is intended to calm you down when you're struggling with symptoms of stress, fear, or anxiety. I like to do it when I'm experiencing a moment of panic, worry, or stress that I cannot seem to escape, especially if it's been preventing me from working or living mindfully that day.

Begin by sitting or lying down in a comfortable position. Take a deep breath in, and as you breathe out, slowly close your eyes. Take a few more normal breaths, focusing on the action of breathing, on how your body rises and falls with each and every breath. Now, gently shift your focus away from your breath and to the surface beneath you. Notice how solid the surface is: it's not going anywhere. It's there for you, holding you up. Breathe in, breathe out. You are fully supported at this moment. At this moment, you have nothing that you must do except breathe in and out.

Think of the sky and the air, how they continue to exist around you, to hold you up. Imagine a cool, refreshing breeze. Allow it to caress your skin, to comfort you as you breathe in, breathe out. Allow it to transport you to a warm beach. The sand beneath you is soft but solid, holding you up. The water's temperature is just right. Imagine the ocean, its waves moving in with every intake of breath and out as you exhale. The waves are washing over you, massaging you, smoothing the rough sand of your body.

Take your time. You still have a few minutes left. The sky is still blue, the Earth is still spinning, everything is okay. All you have to do is breathe in, breathe out. Stay at the beach, stay in the waves, for as long as you need. When you're ready, take one last deep breath in, allow one last wave to wash over you, and as you breathe out, as the water recedes, you are now smooth. Everything is okay.

◇◇◇◇◇◇◇◇◇◇◇◇◇◇◇◇◇◇◇◇◇◇◇◇◇◇◇◇◇◇◇◇◇◇◇◇

What he's looking for, what he wants, is all around him, but he doesn't want that because it is all around him. Every step's an effort, both physically and spiritually, because he imagines his goal to be external and distant.

—Robert M. Pirsig

To just be—to be—amidst all doings, achievings, and becomings. This is the natural state of mind, or original, most fundamental state of being. This is unadulterated Buddha-nature. This is like finding our balance.

—Lama Surya Das

In this moment, there is plenty of time. In this moment, you are precisely as you should be. In this moment, there is infinite possibility.

—Victoria Moran

When you bow, you should just bow; when you sit, you should just sit; when you eat, you should just eat.

—Shunryu Suzuki

When you realize nothing is lacking, the whole world belongs to you.

—Lao Tzu

CHAPTER NINE

Conclusion:

Get Out of Your Head and Back into Your Heart

Because the world we live in today is very much about getting in your head and staying there, many of us have to make a concentrated effort to become grounded and in touch with our bodies and the natural world around us. Grounding is the technique for centering you within your being, getting into your body and out of your head. Grounding is the way we reconnect and balance ourselves though the power of the element of earth. When you see someone driving past talking on their cell phone, you know that they are not grounded. For deep grounding, we recommend a creative visualization or, better yet, a group guided meditation.

This is the simplest of rituals; one you can do every day of your life. As you walk, take the time to look and really see what is in your path. For example, my friend Eileen takes a bag with her and picks up every piece of garbage in her path. She does this as an act of love for the Earth. During the ten years she has practiced this ritual, she has probably turned a mountain of garbage into recycled glass, paper, and plastic. Eileen is very grounded. She is also a happy person who exudes and shares joy to all in her path.

A Month of Mindfulness

◇◇◇◇◇◇◇◇◇◇◇◇◇◇◇◇◇◇◇◇◇◇◇◇◇◇◇◇◇◇◇◇◇◇◇◇

Dear Reader,

These journaling pages are intended to provide you with the space and place to write down your contemplations as you ponder your inner self. When you are emptying your mind in meditation, you can note down some of those thoughts right here. May you receive much inspiration and even more peace of mind on your mindfulness journey.

◇◇◇◇◇◇◇◇◇◇◇◇◇◇◇◇◇◇◇◇◇◇◇◇◇◇◇◇◇◇◇◇◇◇◇◇

What draws you to pursue a more mindful way of life?

After a month of living mindfully, how do you see yourself?

◇◇◇◇◇◇◇◇◇◇◇◇◇◇

What are your spiritual goals?

What are the qualities you desire from this path?

◇◇◇◇◇◇◇◇◇◇◇◇◇◇◇◇◇◇◇◇◇◇◇◇◇

How do you feel after meditating?

◇◇◇◇◇◇◇◇◇◇◇◇◇◇◇◇◇◇◇◇

Have you tried walking meditation? How was your experience?

◇◇◇◇◇◇◇◇◇◇◇◇◇◇◇◇◇◇◇

Which works better for you, morning or evening contemplation?

◇◇◇◇◇◇◇◇◇◇◇◇◇◇◇◇◇◇◇◇◇◇◇◇◇◇◇

Do you pray?

Write down a prayer or hope for your day.

◇◇◇◇◇◇◇◇◇◇◇◇◇◇

Do you long for a "lightness of being"?

◇◇◇◇◇◇◇◇◇◇◇

When do you feel your calmest?

◇◇◇◇◇◇◇◇◇◇◇◇◇◇◇

Do you encounter "monkey mind" and wandering thoughts while meditating?

◇◇◇◇◇◇◇◇◇◇◇◇◇◇◇◇◇◇◇◇◇◇◇◇◇◇◇◇◇◇◇◇◇

What are those thoughts and how can you overcome them?

◇◇◇◇◇◇◇◇◇◇◇◇◇◇◇◇◇◇◇◇◇◇◇◇◇◇◇◇◇◇◇◇◇◇◇◇◇

What keeps you up at night?

What is your favorite kind of meditation?

◇◇◇◇◇◇◇◇◇◇◇◇◇◇◇◇

Do you feel differently on the days which you meditate than the days you do not? If so, how?

◇◇◇◇◇◇◇◇◇◇◇◇

Do people respond to you differently when you meditate regularly? How so?

◇◇◇◇◇◇◇◇◇◇◇◇◇◇◇◇◇◇◇◇◇◇

Does meditation help you when you feel anxiety or worry?

◇◇◇◇◇◇◇◇◇◇◇◇◇◇◇◇◇◇◇◇

Worry is often completely unfounded. How can you stop worrying?

◇◇◇◇◇◇◇◇◇◇◇◇◇◇◇◇◇

What are your fears and how can you handle them?

◇◇◇◇◇◇◇◇◇◇◇◇◇◇◇◇◇◇◇◇◇◇◇◇

Meditation is very good for your brain. What do you notice about yourself in that regard?

◇◇◇◇◇◇◇◇◇◇◇◇◇◇

People who meditate often are much sharper and more focused. Is your thinking more clear after several sessions?

What are you grateful for in your life?

◇◇◇◇◇◇◇◇◇

What personal qualities would you like to develop more of in the future?

◇◇◇◇◇◇◇◇◇◇◇◇

What service can you bring to the world?

◇◇◇◇◇◇◇◇◇◇◇

What does peace of mind look like for you?

◇◇◇◇◇◇◇◇◇◇◇◇

What does a more peaceful world look like?

◇◇◇◇◇◇◇◇◇◇◇◇◇◇◇◇◇◇

What are your personal goals around mindfulness?

◇◇◇◇◇◇◇◇◇◇◇◇◇◇◇◇◇◇◇◇◇◇◇

Where do you see yourself a year from now?

◇◇◇◇◇◇◇◇◇◇◇◇◇◇◇◇

Five years from now?

What inspires you?

◇◇◇◇◇◇◇◇◇◇◇◇◇◇◇◇◇◇◇◇◇

How can you inspire others?

About the Authors

Becca Anderson comes from a long line of preachers and teachers from Ohio and Kentucky. An avid collector of meditations, prayers, and blessings, she helps run a "Gratitude and Grace Circle" that meets monthly at homes, churches, and bookstores. Becca Anderson credits her spiritual practice with helping her recover from cancer and wants to share this with anyone who is facing difficulty in their life. Author of *The Book of Awesome Women* and *Every Day Thankful*, Becca Anderson shares her inspirational writings at http://bloggingyourblessings.blogspot.com/

Elise Marie Collins is an internationally known yogini and instructor on embodied mindfulness. Elise's writing combines her love of ancient healing arts and scientific inquiry. She is currently instructing participants in a two year study on the effects of restorative yoga and stretching for metabolic syndrome. She's the author of *Chakra Tonics: Essential Elixirs for Mind, Body, and Spirit* and *Super Ager: You Can Look Younger, Have More Energy, a Better Memory, and Live a Long and Healthy Life*. Elise Marie Collins teaches yoga at wellness centers all over the great San Francisco Bay Area.

www.ingramcontent.com/pod-product-compliance
Lightning Source LLC
Jackson TN
JSHW071354170426
101040JS00024B/543

* 9 7 8 1 6 3 3 5 3 5 3 1 2 *